HALLOWEEN

HARMLESS FUN or RISKY BUSINESS?

HALLOWEEN

HARMLESS FUN or RISKY BUSINESS?

DIANA WALLIS TAYLOR

WHITAKER
HOUSE

HALLOWEEN:
Harmless Fun or Risky Business?

ISBN: 978-1-62911-164-3
eBook ISBN: 978-1-62911-165-0
Printed in the United States of America
© 2014 by Diana Wallis Taylor

Whitaker House
1030 Hunt Valley Circle
New Kensington, PA 15068
www.whitakerhouse.com

Library of Congress Cataloging-in-Publication Data (Pending)

1 2 3 4 5 6 7 8 9 10   20 19 18 17 16 15 14

CONTENTS

PREFACE

I didn't want to write this book, not because it wasn't needed, but because I knew I would be harassed by the enemy in every way for exposing him.

My introduction to the world of darkness and demonic forces was my grandmother. She lost my grandfather to the influenza epidemic of 1918. An engineer, he had been away on a project, anxious to finish and get home to his family. He assumed he'd contracted a cold and thought he could keep working, but he died within two days. My grandmother was left with three children: my aunt, who was only a year old; my uncle, who was six; and my mother, who was eleven. As the oldest, my mother had known her father longer than any of her siblings and was the most devastated to lose him.

Struggling with the responsibility of three children, my grandmother took a job as a secretary in a dentist's office. She also sought something to heal the loneliness inside, and found a religious group who called themselves the "Ascended Masters," or the "I Am." This was is an offshoot of the Theosophical Society headed by Madame Tingley, a well-known psychic and Spiritualist who built a compound on the site of what is now Point Loma Nazarene University in San Diego, California.

Those who are part of the Ascended Master teachings believe that there is one god, the "Universal All-Pervading Presence of Life," or the "Mighty I Am Presence." Each person is believed to be an incarnation of an "Individualized Presence" of the "Most High Living God"—a part of his or her very own nature and being.[1]

My grandmother had pictures in shades of lavender around her living room of bearded men who looked like prophets. When I inquired about them one day, I was told they were the Ascended Masters. Jesus was one of them. She would go through two hours of "decrees" each morning, praying to each of these "blessed saints" before she started her day. For over forty years, my grandmother wore white on Sundays, went to a "temple," and was a vegetarian. She had a lot of literature, and as a teenager, I read it avidly. I dearly loved my grandmother, and since my family didn't go to church, I thought she was very religious. I even went to the "temple" with her on occasion.

Because of her involvement in this seemingly innocent religion, my sweet little grandmother was demon-possessed

1. http://en.wikipedia.org/wiki/Ascended_master.

in her eighties. She had inadvertently opened a door to the enemy. Within a year or two of her coming to live with my mother, a series of strange events occurred as the enemy began to manifest himself. When my mother went on a vacation with a couple of friends, the caregiver called me in a panic. When I arrived, I found my grandmother out of control, yelling in a strange language, which I finally recognized as her native tongue, Bohemian. My grandmother was a small woman of five feet two inches and weighed about ninety pounds. It took four strong nurses to tie her in restraints. Her gentle hands had soothed my tears; her favorite expression had been "Bless your heart." Now she was cursing and snarling at me from her hospital bed! The eyes looking at me were like dark pools; they were not the eyes of my grandmother. Shocked and terrified, I ran out of the room and spent two hours on the phone calling friend after friend until I tracked down my mother in Sedona, Arizona. "Come home now," I cried into the phone.

My mother divorced my father when I was three years old and my brother was four. She raised her children alone, like my grandmother, and started looking for something to fill the void. This is when she turned to fortune-telling, horoscopes, astrology, books by well-known psychics, and other forms of the occult.

My mother had eventually professed Christ and left the group she'd been involved in, which claimed to be from outer space. She had begun singing in the choir of Kathryn Kuhlman, a well-known healing evangelist in the 1960s. When she returned from Arizona, she took my grandmother, who had calmed down and had finally been released from the hospital, to the next Kathryn Kuhlman service in Los Angeles. My grandmother was healed and delivered that night. She finally discovered who Jesus really was. She was baptized six weeks before she died at the age of ninety. From the glow on her face, I believe that one day I will see her again in heaven.

Like my grandmother, many people who seek peace or spirituality are lured into cults like the Ascended Masters. I am so thankful that my grandmother at last realized that Jesus was not an "ascended master" but the Master of the universe and also her Savior.

Yet my own conversion was a long time coming. I read a lot of books by psychics. Like my mother, I had a curious mind, and I thought that using Chinese fortune sticks and reading horoscopes every day for direction were just fun things to do.

When I was about ten, we moved to a small beach community, and my mother became involved in a spiritualist church in the back canyon, a place associated with the dark arts. She took me along several times, and it frightened me, but I didn't know why. I remember the leader, a woman who called herself a healer, asking for my locket so she could give me a "reading." About the time Mother got involved with them, I had several close calls. I was molested by a plumber who grabbed and French-kissed me when I arrived too early for ballet practice at a local hall and escaped his further intentions by kicking him in the shin and dashing out an open door. I also was nearly kidnapped while walking home one day. I developed a fear of the dark and began to have strange nightmares. It wasn't until years later that I learned that the cause was my mother and my grandmother's dabbling in the occult, which I had no knowledge of at the time.

You see, they had opened the door to the enemy. Satan doesn't care if a person is an innocent child. If you enter his territory, you give him the right to afflict you. My grandmother innocently opened the door when she joined the I Am religion.

My mother told fortunes with a deck of cards to entertain her friends. She taught me how to do this as a child, and I nearly became obsessed with making sure my "fortune" was good each day. We talked about astrology, and we knew all about the zodiac signs. We would find out someone's birthday and look at his zodiac sign to learn his personality and thereby "understand" him.

My mother's intellect and curiosity led her to seek out everything that "interested" her. How I wish that, in my early years, she had sought the Savior who could fill her lonely heart and give her the peace she sought.

I mentioned I had nightmares and feared the dark. The enemy also attracted the wrong men into my life. I was married to an alcoholic for twenty-one years until we divorced. At that point, one of my mother's strong Christian friends told her she needed to pray for me. My mother responded, "I do pray for Diana." The woman looked at her and said, "There is a spirit who sits on her shoulder and brings men into her life who will hurt her."

My mother told me of this conversation, passing it off with a shake of her head. When I got home, out of curiosity, I said out loud, rather flippantly, "So, if you are sitting on my shoulder, what is your name?" Instantly I felt a chill come over me, and the word *loneliness* came to my mind, as clear as if someone had spoken it out loud. Satan doesn't play games.

I was in my thirties and had three children when God delivered me from this spirit. I was invited to a luncheon gathering of Christian women from churches all over the city. After the luncheon, those who wanted prayer were asked to come to the side of the room.

I went over for prayer about a personal situation I was facing. But God had other plans, and the spirit that had been with me since childhood manifested itself. It felt as if steel bands clamped around my chest, and I could hardly breathe. The leader prayed for discernment and was given insight into my problem. She asked me if I had been involved in certain things, and when I said yes, she showed me in the Scriptures how they were abominations to God. I was counseled to renounce them. I did so, naming everything I could think of. The women prayed for me for two hours, and when the enemy was finally exposed, and I had renounced the things of my past, it left me with a sound like a wail.

Fortunately, I was able to go to the home of my Bible teacher and friend, who carefully explained to me what I had experienced. She showed me the many instances in the New Testament where Jesus dealt with demon spirits.

This is why I feel so strongly that it is wrong for Christians to participate in Halloween. As believers, we must consider what we associate with. As the saying goes, "the eyes are the windows of the soul"; so what do we see? What are we allowing into our minds? And, most important, what will be the consequences of our dabbling in areas that belong to the enemy?

As Christians, each of us needs to take this issue before God and ask Him what our course of action should be. If we earnestly seek His will, God will make it clear. His Word is full of direction for our future. It is a love letter from our heavenly Father to each of us. Do we know when the end of the world will come? No. Do we know what will happen tomorrow, next week, or next year? No. But we do know who holds the future. In Jeremiah 29:11, God tells us that He has plans for us, to give us a future and a hope. When my mind turns with questions about what will happen in different circumstances, I've learned to take them to my heavenly Father and leave them at His feet. He shows me the answers—in His time, not mine.

And I have also learned that God is patient. He does not show us all our sins at once, lest we be overwhelmed, and He does not condemn us. As a loving Father, He clearly shows us in His Word what is sin. Then it is our responsibility to acknowledge and renounce our sin. This is what I had to do after He delivered me from the spirit that had been with me from childhood. As you read this book, I pray that your eyes will be opened and your heart will be receptive to the Holy Spirit's leading.

INTRODUCTION

While passing through a shopping mall a few years ago, I noticed a poster in a vacant store window advertising a Halloween costume company coming that September. On the poster was the face of an evil green monster and Dracula with his famous bared fangs. It made me shudder. There were no little costumed children trick-or-treating. A ghost hovered in the background, but he didn't look anything like *Casper the Friendly Ghost* of my children's childhood.

For most people across the United States, including Christians, the word *Halloween* conjures up visions of young children trick-or-treating—showing at their door with bags, plastic pumpkins, or pillowcases held out for a "treat." Homemade costumes used to be the order of the day, and people gave out apples, candy, freshly baked cookies, popcorn balls, or treats to their young nighttime visitors. Unfortunately, a few mentally deranged or simply malicious people hid razor blades in apples or baked a little marijuana into the cookies; due to safety reasons, it became more acceptable to hand out commercial candy.

I participated in Halloween for many years when my children were young, and for years after, I tried handing out homemade cookies along with Christian tracts to those who came to my door. When the number of children exceeded my capacity of cookie baking, I started handing out candy bars with the tracts. Soon it seemed there were more teenagers than small children, and they did very little in the way of costumes. The tracts were tossed on the front lawn. They just wanted the candy. It became too much, and so the next year, we turned off the porch light and left the dark house to go out for a quiet, leisurely dinner.

The past two years, one of our neighbors has gone all out to entertain the kids on Halloween. It is quite a show, with a "live" E.T. rising from a bed, strobe lights with scary music, and spiders and ghosts. Last year, children came by the dozens, and, with the advantage of texting, I presume they invited all their friends. From what I heard, it was a great party, but the hosts ran out of candy around eight thirty, overwhelmed by over 250 trick-or-treaters!

In 2013, the National Retail Association, which keeps track of American consumer spending, estimated that 158 million people would participate in Halloween spending in 2013. The average American would spend around $75.03. Total spending, including costumes, candy, and decorations, was expected to reach 6.9 billion dollars. Of that, some 330 million would be spent to outfit our four-legged friends.[2] Among children, the most popular costumes were princesses, Batman, and animals; among adults were Dracula and zombies.

So when did a seemingly harmless holiday become a night of horror and the epitome of everything evil? The truth is that it didn't *eventually* become evil. Halloween has always represented the forces of darkness, which are disguised in many ways.

For years, I had a nagging feeling in my heart that I needed to forgo celebrating Halloween. But why? It took me a while to finally realize that the Lord was convicting me of celebrating a holiday that does not honor Him.

When the subject of Halloween came up at my daughter's home, my twelve-year-old granddaughter was surprised when I said I ignored the holiday. "What is wrong with celebrating Halloween?" she asked. I decided to research the basic origins of Halloween customs and share them with her. I will share many of my findings in this book, some of which surprised even me. The sources are listed at the back.

If by what I share, including my own experiences, I can reach one family with the reasons for not celebrating this darkest of days, it would be worth all the time gathering this information.

2. https://www.nrf.com/modules.php?name=News&op=viewlive&sp_id=1668.

THE HISTORY OF HALLOWEEN

Halloween has never been a religious holiday like Christmas or Easter. It has always encompassed witchcraft, pagan rituals, and strange beliefs, with a few Christian customs thrown in the mix. Some Christian groups call it the "devil's birthday." It began as a pagan New Year's celebration and evolved into a harvest festival, a merchant's heyday, a time for fall parties and a chance for children to satiate themselves with candy.

Historians believe that Halloween began with a group of people called the Celts, who came from Asia and settled in northern France and the British Isles. They mined, farmed, worked with metals, built roads, used medicine, and had a legal system, among other things. Their priestly class was the Druids. While they worshipped hundreds of deities, they did not keep written records. Some inscriptions in Greek, Latin, and Irish—much of which was recorded by early Christian monks—reveal some information about their celebrations and festivals. They were skilled in the occult arts (the word *occult* means something secret or hidden from those with ordinary knowledge) and worshipped nature, attributing supernatural qualities to it. They also believed that they could be reborn as animals.

They worshipped over four hundred gods, including the sun god, Belenus, and the lord of the dead, Samhain, the chief Druid deity. The former was worshiped on May 1, and the latter on October 31, and both were times for human sacrificing. The victims were chosen by lot in the form of bits of cake handed out to the people. The piece with the black bottom, deliberately burned beforehand, identified the hapless victim who was to be offered to the gods to insure the fertility of their herds, a good harvest, or victory when they went to war.

The holiday of Samhain was a time to settle debts and to pay taxes, much like our tax day, April 15. It was the end of summer and the beginning of winter. They gathered up their crops and brought in their livestock from the fields. They slaughtered their cattle and pigs to serve as food for the winter, leaving only their breeding stock alive for the next year.

The Celts considered certain fruits, legumes, plants, and trees to be holy, including apples, acorns, and hazelnuts.

The Celts gathered at Tara, the seat of ancient kings, for playing sports, paying taxes, and delivering justice to those guilty of crimes. Those who were found guilty of particularly grave crimes were executed.

Before the eve of Samhain, the Celts extinguished their home hearth fires and constructed bonfires on a nearby hill. Embers from these fires were distributed to each household, and a tax was collected for the service. In the days leading up to the Celtic New Year, young children would approach their neighbors and ask them to donate materials to fuel these fires, which were known to ward off evil spirits and "rejuvenate" the sun.[3]

The Druids believed in an afterlife, and that on the night before the New Year, October 31, the door was opened to the underworld. The Celtic day began when the sun went down; so, as darkness fell on October 31, the people began the ceremonies honoring Samhain, the lord of the dead. They believed that on this night, the dead came back to life and that fairylike creatures crossed over into the land of the living to bedevil human beings.

Samhain was believed to summon the souls of the dead who had committed evil and had been condemned to enter the bodies of animals. It was on this sacred day that Samhain decided which souls would advance, in a sense, by being reincarnated as humans, and which ones would remain in the bodies of animals. The Druids believed they could lessen the punishment heaped on their loved ones by praying and offering sacrifices to Samhain.

Furthermore, on this night, Samhain allowed the souls of those who had died the previous year to return to earth for a few hours to associate once more with their families. As a result, the Celts taught that on October 31, ghosts, evil

3. Ankerberg, John, John Weldon, and Dillon Burroughs, *The Facts on Halloween* (Eugene, OR: Harvest House Publishers, 1996, 2008), 10.

spirits, and witches roamed the earth. Large bonfires were lit to frighten away these demonic spirits, which were believed to play tricks on humans and cause supernatural manifestations. People dressed up in animal skins to chase away the spirits and wild animals that might try to approach them during the celebration. This practice may have been the beginning of the tradition of dressing in costume on Halloween. Women dressed as men, and men dressed as women, to fool the evil spirits. Others put on grotesque masks and danced around these great bonfires, pretending to be chased by evil spirits, or the evil dead. Some people would dress in masks and costumes to "trick" evil spirits into thinking they were someone else, so that they would leave them and their townsfolk alone. But they would set out food and drinks to welcome the good souls.

At the time of this New Year, fortune-telling and divination (the magic art of interpreting the unknown from random patterns and symbols) were prevalent. The feast of Samhain was a holiday to peer into the future, to divine fate, and to communicate with the supernatural. One way they foretold the future was by sacrificing animals and observing their innards.

When the Romans conquered the Celts, they brought their own gods and goddesses with them, and many of their customs were blended with the Celts'. Yet these ancient English communities did not want to give up their pagan festivals.

Around 600 BC, in the Dark Ages and early Middle Ages, Catholicism grew as priests, including Saint Patrick (who Christianized Ireland), began to spread Christianity throughout the Celtic world. The Roman Catholic Church soon became the authority in the land. It opposed these pagan festivals and soon found that it was easier to convert the Celts by offering them alternatives. Pope Gregory III changed the date of the feast of the martyrs to November 1, the date of Samhain, and indicated that it was to be a celebration of all the saints of the church, not just the martyrs. So, the Church sought to replace pagan customs by making November 1 All Saints' Day, and November 2 All Souls' Day. The pope felt it would make the change from pagan religion to Christianity a little easier on the people. He permitted new converts to keep some of their pagan feasts, but from then on, they would be celebrated as "Christian" feasts. Instead of praying to their pagan gods, they were now admonished to remember the deaths of the saints and to pray for them in order to help them escape the torments of purgatory (a place where deceased sinners go to be rid of their sins prior to going to heaven).

Some of these beliefs live on in the customs of various cultures surrounding All Saints' Day and All Souls' Day.

Catholics believe that they could save their deceased loved ones from suffering in purgatory by praying and giving alms on their behalf, similar to the "indulgences" that could be purchased from the church for this purpose in the Middle Ages.

The Druids believed in something like purgatory, as mentioned earlier, and that the sinful souls of those who had died and had been relegated to the bodies of animals could be freed to enter heaven by their gifts and sacrifices. Only Samhain could judge these souls and decree what form of body, whether of a human being or an animal, they could inhabit.

On All Souls' Day in Belgium, people eat special "all souls' cakes" and believe that with each one they eat, they save a soul from purgatory. In Sicily, they eat cakes that resemble skulls and skeletons. In France, people pray for those who are in purgatory.

First John 1:9 tells us, *"If we confess our sins, He is faithful and just to forgive us our sins and to cleanse us from all unrighteousness."* The Scriptures tell us that no human being, no matter how holy they are, has the power to forgive our sins, only God.

On the "Day of All Saints," November 1, the church service or mass was celebrated as "Allhallowmas." The night before this mass was called "All Hallowed Evening." It became "All Hallows' Eve," and then, when "All" was dropped, it was shortened to "Halloween." Again, it was a deliberate attempt to replace the pagan holiday of Samhain with a Christian holiday. The priests encouraged their parishioners to remember the dead with prayers rather than sacrifices. The first recorded Roman Catholic celebration of Halloween was the "Festyvall" of 1511 in England. Special foods were baked, a custom already common in the land, and were given to Christian souls.

There has been controversy among historians over how much Samhain really contributed to the modern celebration of Halloween, but a study of the Celtic festivals, pagan rites, and beliefs shows how much of this holiday is retained in our present celebrations.

After Henry VIII ascended the throne of England in 1509, he wanted a divorce, which is forbidden by the Catholic Church. So, he started the Church of England to separate from the Vatican. Both he and his daughter Queen Elizabeth I considered All Saints' Day a papal holiday and tried issuing proclamations to eradicate it. Bell ringers continued a superstitious ringing of the bells on All Hallows'

Eve, starting in the evening and lasting all night long. Henry VIII tried fining them, but the bells continued to ring as the people perpetuated their occult beliefs.

While the church intended Halloween to be a holy evening, it has become a night that is anything but holy. It may not be as harmless and innocent as some assume it to be. Many people say, "Well, that was long ago. We don't do all those things in this day and age. Halloween is just a fun holiday for kids."

But is it really? Let's take a look at some similar customs associated with Halloween that are celebrated around the world.

2

MODERN-DAY DRUIDS

While researching information on the ancient Druids, I learned, to my surprise, that there is a group of people who still carry on their ancient traditions. They are called the Stonehenge and Amesbury Druids.

Below is a description of these Druids, according to their Web site:

> As an ancient pagan religion, our belief is based on the reverential, sacred and honourable relationship between the people and the land. In its personal expression, it is the spiritual interaction between an individual and the spirits of nature, including those

of landscape and ancestry, together with the continuities of spiritual, literary and cultural heritage.[4]

These modern-day Druids state that those who practice Druidry have a deep spiritual connection with the British land and culture, and that their practices continue to gain popularity around the world. They acknowledge and worship many supreme beings, including natural forces, such as thunder, the sun, and the earth, as well as spirits of place, like mountains, rivers, and divine guides.

Stonehenge and Amesbury Druids say that Druidry cannot be defined or limited to the reverence of one deity or a pantheon. Some worship Celtic deities; others worship Saxon, Nordic, or Classical deities; and still others worship animistic and conceptual forms of supreme beings.

For many years, a great amount of attention has been focused on the "crop circles" that have seemingly appeared overnight in farmers' fields. Speculation of the culprits ranges from groups of pranksters to aliens. The intricate design of these works has caused many to wonder just how in the world they came about. In studying this phenomenon, it was discovered that many of these mysterious circles are found within the territory of the ruins we know as Stonehenge, which is attributed to the Druids. However, Stonehenge was built around 2400 BC, and the Druids arrived around 1500 BC. Stonehenge and Amesbury Druids of today claim that there was already a very sophisticated spiritual process in Britain long before that the Celts arrived, and the Celts, instead of conquering the people of the land, merely merged with them. Thus, while the Celts did not build Stonehenge, it became part of their rituals.

---

4. http://www.stonehenge-druids.org/druids.html.

Modern-day Druids believe that their ancestors wrote in Greek and ogham.[5] They also believe that their forefathers were not allowed to write down their customs, rites, and lore. Their wisdom had to be learned by memory, so that it could be passed down orally through the generations. According to the group's Web site, it could take up to twenty years of study.

Thus, the ancient customs of the Celts and their priests, the Druids, still exist today. Their religion apparently is not only of the past; rather, according to these present-day Druids, it is actually growing in many places around the world.

In the next chapter, we will explore yet another festival with pagan origins that is practiced to this day.

5. ogham: the alphabetic system of fifth and sixth century Irish in which an alphabet of 20 letters is represented by notches for vowels and lines for consonants and which is known principally from inscriptions cut on the edges of rough standing tombstones.

3

THE DAY OF THE DEAD

One of the biggest celebrations honoring the dead is called *Día de los Muertos* (Day of the Dead). Celebrated in Mexico, this festival originated more than three thousand years ago.

The festival that became the Day of the Dead was celebrated in the ninth month of the Aztec calendar and continued for thirty days. Dedicated to the goddess Catrina, the "Lady of the Dead," it is a day when people honor their ancestors, family, and friends. Día de los Muertos involves an ancient ritual of the living communing with the dead—"a mystical night when the veil is supposedly lifted between the realms of life and death, so that family members and friends can share a day together."[6] Those who celebrate this festival consider it to be one of the holiest celebrations in the cycle of life.

On November 1, *Día de los Santos Inocentes* (Day of the Holy Innocents) or *Día de los Angelitos* (Day of the Little Angels), people remember and honor deceased children and infants.

On October 31, All Hallows' Eve, the children make an altar to invite the *angelitos* (spirits of the dead children) to come back for a visit. On November 1, All Saints' Day, the spirits of the deceased adults are said to come to visit. On November 2, in most regions of Mexico, families go to the cemetery to decorate the tombs and graves of their relatives. During this three-day fiesta, marigolds, the flowers of the dead, abound. *Pan de los Muerto*, "Bread of the Dead," is a sweet, yeasty egg bread served during the festivities. The bread is formed into various shapes, from skulls to rabbits, and decorated with white frosting to look like twisted bones. Skulls of sugar or chocolate, cardboard skeletons, tissue-paper decorations, fruit and nuts, incense, and other paraphernalia, fill the homes and marketplaces in Mexico.

An artist by the name of José Guadalupe Posada (1852–1913) created a famous print of a figure he called *La Calavera Catrina*, or "The Elegant Skull." This costumed female skull has become associated with the Day of the Dead and is often a prominent part of modern observances of the holiday. Assorted figurines and other items reflecting her image are found in most Mexican shops during and after the month of October. Shrines to Calavera Catrina are built in homes, schools, and even government offices, marking this as an important holiday in the Latino world.

---

6. www.ladayofthedead.com/history.html.

In Guatemala, this day is observed by the flying of giant kites and by visits to ancestors' graves. In Ecuador, the holiday is observed mostly by poorer people. They gather at the local cemetery with offerings of ceremonial food and beverages like *colada morada*, a spiced fruit drink that gets its purple color from Andean blackberries and purple corn flour. It is eaten with bread shaped like a baby wrapped in swaddling clothes.

In Haiti, *vodou* (Haitian spelling of *voodoo*) traditions are mixed with Roman Catholic observances. Loud drums and other musical instruments are played all night at cemeteries to awaken Baron Samedi, the *loa* (spirit) of the dead, and his mischievous family of offspring, the "Gede."

Artistic renderings of Baron Samedi portray him as a corpse, ready for burial, with a top hat, black tuxedo, dark glasses, and cotton plugs in his nose, hence his nasal voice.

The loa are the spirits of Haitian vodou, also called "mystères" or the "invisibles." They are intermediaries between *Bon Dieu*, or the "good god," the "creator," who is far removed from the world, and human beings. Each loa is considered to have its own distinct personality, marked by unique songs, dances, rhythms, and symbols. They are not prayed to, but they are served by those who worship them. Baron Samedi is also considered the "loa of resurrection." Haitians believe he has the power to heal a person of any disease or condition and that he is the only one who can usher a soul into the underworld.

Baron Samedi is believed to give life, and Haitians attribute the power of vodou curses and black magic to him. It is also believed that he asks for and receives gifts of cigars, rum, black coffee, grilled peanuts, and bread. A vodou ceremony is usually required to summon him from the underworld to this world.

Sadly, while the people acknowledge a creator, they do not acknowledge the Savior, the One whom they must face one day, and the only One who can truly impart eternal life.

Other South American countries and some American communities of Hispanic residents celebrate Día de los Muertos in a way that is very similar to Mexican tradition. Inhabitants of Old Town San Diego, California, celebrate this holiday for two full days and end their festivities with a candlelight procession to El Campo Santo Cemetery. The day is also celebrated in Prague, Czech Republic, and the Philippines, among other countries.

One of the biggest celebrations of Día de los Muertos occurs at Hollywood Forever Cemetery in Los Angeles, California. Founded in 1899, it is considered the oldest memorial park in California. Given its proximity to Paramount Studios, it is no surprise that celebrities are buried there, especially movie actors and directors, including John Huston, Darren McGavin, Cecil B. DeMille, Douglas Fairbanks, and Charlie Chaplin.

For the last fourteen years, the cemetery has opened its gates to annually commemorate Día de los Muertos. As their brochure advertises, "[It is] in the spirit of the goddess Mictecacihuatl, known as the 'Lady of the Dead,' and Samhain, the Celtic day feast of the dead....[It is a day] to call upon the living to engage and summons [sic] the spirits of our lives who shaped, inspired and left their prints engraved in our souls."[7] To commemorate the dead, visitors construct altars and give offerings, such as marigolds and incense, which give off aromas that are believed to attract the

7. http://www.ladayofthedead.com/history.html.

dead to the place of the feast. They set out photos, food, and other items to welcome their deceased family members and friends, and they carry candles, which are believed to "illuminate the shadows of death."[8]

Does this sound familiar? Once again, festivals like Día de los Muertos show that many ancient rituals are still with us.

Even though some Christian concepts have been mixed with the ancient rituals of this holiday, the fact that Christ died for us and rose again, that we might have eternal life through Him, is not included in any way. As much as we would wish it, we cannot bring our loved ones back from the dead. We can only look forward to the resurrection, when we have the hope of seeing again those who died knowing Christ.

The Scriptures tell us, *"When men tell you to consult mediums and spiritists, who whisper and mutter, should not a people inquire of their God? Why consult the dead on behalf of the living?"* (Isaiah 8:19 NIV).

Ephesians 5:11 tells us to *"have no fellowship with the unfruitful works of darkness, but rather expose them."*

First Timothy 2:5 (NLT) says, *"For there is only one God and one Mediator who can reconcile God and humanity—the man Christ Jesus."*

A wise man once said, "Our life is not determined by the dreams we dream but the choices we make." We must make the choice to follow Christ in this life if we would live eternally. All the offerings in the world cannot decide the fate of those who have gone before us.

---

8. Ibid.

4

GHOULS AND ZOMBIES

Part of the belief in zombies, or the walking dead, comes from Africa and Haiti. In Haitian vodou, a "bokor," or sorcerer, can revive a dead person and control him, because he does not have a will his own. In the seventeenth and eighteenth centuries, Haitians believed that Baron Samedi had the power to bring dead people back from the grave and take them to heaven. If they had made him upset, they would remain a slave, or a "zombie."

The word *zombi*, of West African vodun (voodoo), is the name of the vodou snake Damballah, and comes from the Kikongo word *nzambi*, which means "god." The part of the

37

soul that is controlled by the bokor is called a zombie "astral." The bokor usually keeps the astral inside a bottle and sells it to clients for luck, healing, or business success. Some believe that this state is only temporary and that after a time, God repossesses the soul. Legends of vodou hold that feeding zombies salt will make them return to their graves. In parts of South Africa, some people believe witches can turn people into zombies by killing them and possessing their bodies, thereby forcing them to become slaves.[9]

In 1937, someone researching folklore in Haiti was unable to come up with any conclusive information on a woman who claimed to have been dead. There was evidence of the use of psychoactive drugs, but no one would offer information on this.[10]

Years later, the ethnobotanist Wade Davis published his findings on zombies in *The Serpent and the Rainbow* (1985) and *Passage of Darkness: The Ethnobiology of the Haitian Zombie* (1988). During his time in Haiti investigating zombies, he discovered that "a living person can be turned into a zombie by two special powders being introduced into the blood stream (usually via a wound)...includ[ing] tetrodotoxin (TTX), a powerful and frequently fatal neurotoxin found in the flesh of the pufferfish.... The second powder consists of dissociate drugs such as datura. Together, these powders were said to induce a deathlike state in which the will of the victim would be entirely subjected to that of the bokor [sorcerer]."[11]

Later research concludes that these powders can cause numbness, nausea, and paralysis of the diaphragm, but they do not produce the deathlike trance and rigid walking so

9. http://en.wikipedia.org/wiki/Zombie.
10. Ibid.
11. Ibid.

often portrayed in zombie movies. Other research shows that Davis's report has some credulity.[12]

Zombies are "in" these days. Movies and television programs such as *The Walking Dead* are having a field day making people look like zombies stumbling around. Zombie costumes were in high demand last Halloween. Once again, we like to be scared out of our minds, or so the filmmakers would have us believe.

But there are no "walking dead," people who come up out of the grave to haunt us. We have one life, which is lived here on earth. After we leave this world and are buried, we cannot come out of our graves to scare people. We come out of our graves only at the resurrection, when we stand before Christ, our righteous Judge.

12. Ibid.

5

TRICK OR TREAT

For most children today, trick-or-treating is what Halloween is all about. We've heard those three words a thousand times from little costumed persons on our porches. But where did the phrase come from?

As a child, I loved the "treat" aspect of Halloween as much as any other child. I dressed up with my brother and friends, and we took our pillowcases or paper bags around to collect as much candy as we could. Like many children, we made ourselves sick on candy, oblivious to the origins of our annual foray into the neighborhood.

To learn the real story behind trick-or-treating, we must again go back to the Middle Ages. On the eves of All Saints' Day, November 1, and All Souls' Day, November 2, people went "mumming," or "guising," which consists of parading in costume, chanting rhymes, and playacting. This custom was originally associated with Christmas but was later attributed to Halloween.

Going "a-souling" meant going from door to door and offering prayers for the dead in exchange for treats. These treats were generally in the form of "soul cakes" and other sweets. In the 1880s, children in Great Britain and Ireland would go around to the houses on All Saints' Day and sing a little song (also called "souling"). Here are two versions I found:

> Soul day, soul day,
> We be come a-souling;
> Pray, good people, remember the poor,
> And give us all a soul cake.
> One for Peter, two for Paul,
> Three for Him who made us all.
> An apple, a pear, a plum, or a cherry,
> Or any good thing to make us merry.
> Soul day, soul day,
> We have been praying
> For the soul departed:
> So pray, good people, give us a cake,
> For we are all poor people,
> Well known to you before;
> So give us a cake for charity's sake,
> And our blessing we'll leave at your door.[13]

13. Quoted in the newspaper *Bilston Mercury*.

Soul! soul! a soul-cake!
Good mistress; gi' us a soul-cake!
One for Peter; one for Paul;
And one for Them [sic] as made us all.
An apple or a cherry
Or anything else to make us merry!
Go! good mistress! to the cellar;
And fetch us a pail o' water.
It is a good fame
To get a good name.[14]

In Britain, youths wearing masks and sometimes carrying carved turnips lighted by live coals begged for pennies. In Ireland, farmers went from house to house, asking for food in the name of their ancient gods. The food was to be used for the village Halloween celebration. Good luck or physical treats were promised to those who supplied goodies. "Give us something, or we will trick you," they would threaten those whom they petitioned for treats.

In the mid-1800s, the potato blight in Ireland caused so many crops to fail that there wasn't enough food for families to eat. Irish immigrants fled to America to escape the great potato famine. They came by the thousands, searching for a better life, and they brought their own Halloween traditions to the United States. Half a million Scottish immigrants also brought their own Halloween customs to America. By then, mumming, or souling, was generally forgotten, and no one gave out soul cakes; but Halloween was soon pretty well established here.

In 1870, an article in *Godey's Lady's Book* portrayed Halloween as a holiday for English children. It talked of children entering a house by stepping over a broom in order to

---

14. *The Cheshire Sheaf*, 1896.

keep witches out. Then they would tell fortunes by various means, including pouring hot lead into water and "reading" the shapes that were formed. There were taffy pulls and the making of "fate" cakes, which were small pastries prepared and baked in silence and then put under a pillow to invoke dreams. The article was widely read, and it stimulated many readers to have similar parties of their own.

In the 1920s, many towns were compelled to devise ways to discourage the growing trend of vandalism. Some methods involved organizing parades and contests for the citizenry. When the Great Depression hit, few families had extra money to spend, and one of the solutions was for neighbors to pool their resources and create one organized Halloween party. Groups of children were led from one house to the next, each home hosting a different activity. This event soon evolved into the popular tradition of trick-or-treating as we know it today, when children go from house to house asking for treats.

There was a custom similar to trick-or-treating among the Pennsylvania Dutch communities called *Pelznickel*, from the German word *pelzen* ("to wallop") and the German name *Nikolaus*. In areas of the US and Canada, groups of costumed participants moved from house to house offering small "tricks" in exchange for treats of food and drink. Nickel was portrayed as a crotchety old man dressed in ragged furs or old dirty clothes who came to houses in the community a week or two before Christmas. He carried a switch in his hand, supposedly to be used to beat bad children. The children were never beaten but were frightened enough to be good so that Saint Nicolas would bring them presents on Christmas. The figure also carried a bag over his shoulder, and if the children sang a song or answered his riddle, he would throw candy on the floor.

By the end of the World War II, when rationing was over, commercial candy was more readily available, and the modern custom of trick-or-treating finally spread throughout America.

Many people believed that evil spirits roamed the earth on Halloween, playing pranks on the living; therefore, people wore masks and costumes to avoid detection by them. It was not long before people began playing tricks on their neighbors and friends, attributing these pranks to the evil spirits. This sounds a lot like what happens today.

My first memory of Halloween is from when I was five years old, waiting for my mother on the steps of my kindergarten classroom. In my lap was an old sheet with two holes cut out for my eyes. I was to be a ghost. My mother, who didn't believe clocks served any good purpose, was always late, and I despaired that the school carnival would be over before she got there. When at last she arrived, the first thing we did was go through the "haunted house." It was a converted cloakroom, darkened, with eerie sounds, fake spider webs, and people jumping out at you with scary faces. I was a timid child, and this experience was terrifying to me. I remember sobbing so hysterically that my mother had to rush me outside.

Recalling that traumatic experience, it saddens me to see well-meaning organizations, even church youth groups, set up "haunted houses" each year, giving them such names as "The House of Horror" or "The Evil Castle." While the Haunted Mansion is a popular attraction at Disneyland, I got a strange feeling going through it. I couldn't wait to get out.

Some people seem to enjoy being scared out of their wits. Some emerge from haunted houses without ill effects, but there are thousands who retain the fear and terror generated by these experiences. Small children do not know how to handle someone dressed as Dracula with dripping fangs or Frankenstein leaping out from the darkness. That fear can remain for years, as it did with me. I find myself wondering why many parents, most of whom are usually so protective of their children, dress them up as little witches, ghosts, mummies, or devils, when their children have no idea what these costumes represent.

In the 1940s and 1950s, merchants began to capitalize on the practice of trick-or-treating by selling elaborate costumes and other related products. In the past, costumes had been rather simple; popular choices were characters whose outfits could be assembled using old clothing, such as pirates, gypsies, hoboes, or bandits. But in the 1950s, when cheap rayon, vinyl, and plastic became available, the production of cheap masks and commercial costumes soared. It was no longer popular to be a ghost, using an old sheet, as I had done in kindergarten. Now people wanted to dress like popular movie stars and, later, like figures from television shows and movies, such as *Star Wars* and *Frankenstein*. Ghoulish masks and costumes became more and more graphic and scary. One benefit of the new merchandising is the flame-retardant materials used.

As manufacturers sought to capitalize further on the holiday, Halloween cartoons appeared in magazines, and other commercial items became available, such as noisemakers, plastic pumpkins, and other paraphernalia.

The biggest appeal of Halloween for children may be that, for one night of the year, they are allowed to put aside their identity, stay out after dark, and be showered with candy by adults at house after house. But what must God think of our children dressed up as ghosts, witches, and devils? Again, we need to seek God's Word for direction.

It says, *"In everything you do, put God first, and he will direct you and crown your efforts with success"* (Proverbs 3:6 TLB).

6

BLACK CAT BONE

Black cats are among the most-often-used figures to represent Halloween. They are an integral part of Halloween posters, often shown hissing, with their backs arched and their fur standing up. Sometimes they are pictured riding with a witch on a broomstick. Many people like cats, so what is the harm?

Many of our superstitions of black cats, such as the one that admonishes us not to cross paths with a black cat to avoid bad luck, derive from the fear of these animals.

Once again, these superstitions date back to the Druids, the ancient priests who believed that on the night before

November 1, Samhain gathered together wicked spirits that had been condemned the year before. Since the Druids feared these spirits, they chose the evening of October 31 to sacrifice to their gods, hoping to protect themselves from these evil spirits. They considered cats to be holy animals, because they represented people who had committed wicked deeds in their lifetime and then were reincarnated as cats after death. Because most cats have a sort of aristocratic air about them, it is easy to understand why people attributed human traits to them.

Today, black cats still seem to represent these evil spirits. During ancient Druid ceremonies, even in the Middle Ages, cats were burned in wicker cages in the November 1 fires—a gruesome thought, but then again, these were pagan peoples with superstitious beliefs.

In the South, black-cat lore ran rampant. The magic of the "black cat bone," a lucky charm used in hoodoo, was a well-known superstition among the African Americans in the nineteenth century. After a period of fasting, they would catch a black cat and boil it alive at midnight; afterward, a hoodooist would examine its bones and identify which one had magic. This is still practiced today, with various methods of determining the "magical" bone. Some stores still sell "black cat bones," but many times, these bones have been found to be chicken bones that have been dyed black. Once again, leading historians have considered that black-cat lore originated with the Druids.

Halloween is a time when there is a large demand for cats, especially black ones. A friend of mine from New Mexico shared with me that a friend of hers, a retired FBI agent, told her he dreaded Halloween because of the increase in crime. He shared another gruesome detail: After Halloween, there

were always reports from officers who had found carcasses of
animals that had been sacrificed in the surrounding hills and
caves. If so, it's a grim reminder that other pagan customs are
still with us.

7

OWLS

The black cat is not the only animal associated with Halloween. The owl, a predator of the night, is also featured. Because of their haunting sounds, owls give the night an eerie feeling.

In the Middle Ages, many people feared owls, thinking they were evil spirits that ate the souls of their dying friends and family members. These birds are also associated with wasteland. Never in the Scriptures is the owl presented in a positive light. Isaiah 34:11 says, *"But the pelican and the porcupine shall possess it* [the wasteland], *also the owl and the raven shall dwell in it. And He shall stretch out over it the line of*

53

confusion and the stones of emptiness." In many cultures, owls are messengers of death and representatives of the underworld. Some believe the owl's cry signals a person's death.

Margaret Craven's book *I Heard the Owl Call My Name* is based on this belief among the Alaskan natives. In the book, a young priest is sent by his superior to work among the indigenous people. He is dying, but he doesn't know it. At the end, just before dying, he hears his own name called by an owl and finally realizes the validity of the local lore he had dismissed as superstition.

Surprisingly, in ancient Greece, the owl was seen as a sign of good fortune. The Romans, however, saw owls as omens of impending disaster and imminent death. Julius Caesar, Augustus, and Agrippa were said to have heard the hoot of an owl before their deaths. While the Greeks believed that the sighting of an owl predicted victory for their armies, the Romans saw it as a sign of defeat. Roman sailors believed that if a person dreamed of an owl, it was an omen of shipwreck and tragedy. To ward off the evil portended by an owl, it was believed that the offending owl should be killed and nailed to the door of the affected house. In America, out of fear, people tried to stop owls from hooting. In Texas, some people would throw salt into a fire, a practice that supposedly protected them from the evil of owls. Ancient Babylonians used owl amulets to protect pregnant women.

Among American Indian tribes, owls were often viewed as harbingers of sickness or death. Still other tribes believed them to be protective spirits. Others thought they were souls of the living dead or recently departed dead, which were to be treated with respect. And still others believed them to be the earthly incarnations of their gods. The Burrowing Owl was considered by the Hopi Indians to be the god of the dead.

In over seventy-five countries around the world, the owl is a negative symbol. In parts of France, owls are believed to help spinsters find a husband. Southeast Asian Indians use food made from owls for their medicinal values, thought to include curing children of seizures, and also as an aphrodisiac. They also believe that the number of times an owl hoots is a predictor of forthcoming events. Over one thousand owls are killed by black magicians in India every year during a ceremony called Diwali, in hopes of warding off bad luck. They also feel they can obtain magical powers from owls.

+ In Africa, the owl is known as the sorcerer's bird—it brings illness to children, and its cry precedes evil.

+ In Germany, if an owl hoots as a child is born, the infant is expected to have an unhappy life.

+ In Ireland, an owl that enters a house must be killed at once, because it is thought to take all of the luck with it if it flies away.

+ In Cameroon, the owl is referred to as "the bird who makes you afraid."

+ Hebrew literature depicts owls as unclean, harbingers of blindness and desolation.

+ In Mexico, the owl is called the "messenger of the lord of the land of the dead," flying between the lands of the living and the dead.

+ The Māori, an indigenous people of New Zealand, consider the owl to be an unlucky bird.

+ Spanish legend holds that the owl was a sweet singer until the day it saw Jesus crucified on the cross. Since then, it has avoided daylight and has always repeated the words "cruz, cruz," meaning "cross, cross."[15]

15. http://www.owlpages.com/articles.php?section=owl+mythology&title=world.

In the book of Leviticus, among the birds the Lord lists as an abomination and not to be eaten are owls. (See Leviticus 11:13–18.) Wherever there is the aftermath of destruction, there are owls.

These beliefs of owls add to the mysterious and frightening superstitions of Halloween. Many Christians collect all sorts of owls, made out of a variety of materials, from wood to paintings, and I have seen large ceramic owls lit by candles set out on porches on Halloween. But do we as God's examples want to showcase such an object of evil superstitions?

8

APPLE BOBBING

Most of us have probably taken part in apple bobbing. It's a favorite game at school carnivals and church "harvest festivals." We laugh, get our faces wet, and generally make fools of ourselves, trying to get our teeth on the slippery apples as they dance away from us.

The game of apple bobbing was popular in Britain for hundreds of years. By the nineteenth century, it was done mostly in Ireland and small parts of England. It is thought that bobbing for apples was a divination game, part of the known customs of Halloween in early times. The origin of apple bobbing is uncertain, but some historians believe it began in the British Isles before the Romans brought Christianity, perhaps in Ireland and Scotland. Because Samhain was celebrated in October, the peak of the apple harvest, there were plenty of them to go around. The use of this game as a means of fortune-telling did not come until many years later.

British writer William Henry Davenport Adams ascribed the divination use of this fruit to "old Celtic fairy lore." Here is how he described apple bobbing:

> [Apples] are thrown into a tub of water, and you endeavour to catch one in your mouth as they bob round and round in provoking fashion. When you have caught one, you peel it carefully, and pass the long strip of peel thrice, *sunwise*, round your head; after which you throw it over your shoulder, and it falls to the ground in the shape of the initial letter of your true love's name.[16]

People had a variety of ways of foretelling a person's future with apples. One involved counting the number of seeds in an apple: two foretold an early marriage, and three revealed future riches. Sometimes, a piece of an apple was put under a person's pillow to encourage prophetic dreams.

"Snap apple" is another game played on Halloween and is very similar to apple bobbing. The only difference is that the apples are tied on a string instead of placed in water. This is why Halloween used to be known as "Snap-Apple Night." The person who got the first bite of apple was predicted to be the first one to marry. At these gatherings, always occurring around Halloween, the guests usually dressed up as witches, ghosts, or goblins.

16. William Henry Davenport Adams, *Curiosities of Superstition, and Sketches of Some Unrevealed Religions* (London: J. Masters and Co., 1882), 293.

Today, apple bobbing still entails trying to capture an apple with your teeth. But the pastime has lost some favor over the years due to sanitary reasons, since each person has to put his head in the same water. It seems to be a simple enough game, with participants playing for a prize instead of to determine their love life, but the truth is that it began as a form of divination.

JACK-O'-LANTERNS AND THE LEGEND OF "IRISH JACK"

9

The seemingly harmless practice of carving pumpkins into what are called jack-o'-lanterns originated with the Celts. They carved turnips and put live coals inside of them to ward off evil spirits. Witches also placed candles inside human skulls and carried them with them on their journey to coven[17] meetings. This may be where the tradition of carving pumpkins originated.

The term "jack-o'-lantern" comes from an old Irish legend of a man known as Stingy Jack. As the story goes,

---

17. coven: an assembly or band of usually 13 witches.

Stingy Jack invited the devil to have a drink with him. True to his name, Stingy Jack didn't want to pay for his drink, so he convinced the devil to turn himself into a coin that Jack could use to buy their drinks. Once the devil did so, Jack decided to keep the money, and he put it into his pocket next to a silver cross. This prevented the devil from changing back into his original form. Jack eventually freed the devil, under the conditions that he would not bother Jack for one year and that, should Jack die, he would not claim his soul.

The next year, Jack again tricked the devil by convincing him to fetch him an apple in a tree. As the devil was climbing the tree, Jack carved a cross into the bark at the trunk to prevent the devil from coming back down. Then the devil was blackmailed, having to promise Jack that he wouldn't claim his soul for at least ten years.

When Jack died, God would not allow him into heaven because of the wicked life he had lived on earth. So Jack went to the devil, but he wouldn't accept him either, keeping the promise he had made. As Jack turned to leave hell, the devil launched a hot coal at him, and, to light his way, Jack put the coal into a carved turnip he'd been eating. Legend has it that ever since, he's been homeless and wandering around with his jack-o'-lantern. Thus, the jack-o'-lantern became the symbol of a lost soul.

In Ireland, a carved turnip or potato was used, but when the Irish came to America, they discovered the pumpkin. The Irish were so afraid of suffering the same fate as Jack that they began to hollow out pumpkins, carve scary faces into them, and place lighted candles inside to scare away evil spirits from their homes. Today, when we carve pumpkins, put candles in them, and use them to decorate for Halloween, are we unconsciously trying to scare away evil spirits? We need to ask ourselves if we should be following customs that started in superstition and fear.

GHOSTS

What would Halloween be without ghosts? From costumes to lawn decorations to candy, ghosts are an iconic part of the holiday. Just as there are marshmallow chicks at Easter, there are now marshmallow ghosts for Halloween.

Many of us are familiar with the cartoon *Casper the Friendly Ghost*. The cute little figure makes ghosts seem like harmless friends. While he had some mean-spirited uncles called the Ghostly Trio, Casper is a "good" ghost who tries to escape the "life" of a spiritual being by befriending humans.

Unfortunately, there aren't any friendly ghosts. As a matter of fact, ghosts don't exist at all.

People claim to have seen ghosts, some believing that they are dead people who cannot rest because they died in a terrible way and that they haunt a certain place for eternity. Movies and television shows love to play on that theme.

In the movie *Ghost*, Patrick Swayze plays the dead victim of a botched mugging. As a ghost, he desperately tries to contact his grieving girlfriend, played by Demi Moore, to warn her she is also in danger. Whoopi Goldberg plays a medium who is the only one who can "see" him and give Moore the message. With Goldberg's help, the villain, Swayze's former partner, is finally killed and hauled off by horrible little demon creatures. In the end, his mission of revenge accomplished, Swayze walks off into a golden light, supposedly representing heaven. Whoopi Goldberg is an example of a medium who entertained a "familiar spirit"—Swayze—who used her body as a tool for his work.

The movie made ghosts and mediums seem believable. However, the scene in which Swayze's partner dies and is hauled off into the darkness by what appear to be imps or demons is closer to the truth than we like to imagine.

For we are not fighting against flesh-and-blood enemies, but against evil rulers and authorities of the unseen world, against mighty powers in this dark world, and against evil spirits in the heavenly places.

(Ephesians 6:12 NLT)

Another popular movie, *Ghostbusters*, is about a group of people who search for ghosts with special equipment and claim to take pictures of these entities. They explore buildings and other places that people claim are haunted. These ghosts, or spirits, are supposedly dead people who came back to haunt the place where they died.

Many ghost stories, including those by American authors, are based on the superstitions and rituals of the ancient Druids. One of the most popular ghost stories in American literature is Washington Irving's *Legend of Sleepy Hollow*, featuring the ghost called the "Headless Horseman." This German ghost lost his head when it was blown off by a cannonball in the war. Ichabod Crane, a schoolteacher, didn't heed the warning about the headless ghost, who was out looking for a new head. The Headless Horseman appeared out of nowhere, nearly running down the terrified Ichabod. Later it is revealed that the "ghost" is really Brom Bones, Ichabod's rival, who is also fighting for the hand of the lovely Katrina van Tassel.

Another popular ghost story is *A Christmas Carol*, by Charles Dickens, in which the ghosts of Christmases Past, Christmas Present, and Christmases Yet to Come haunt a man named Ebenezer Scrooge, prompting him to change his miserly ways.

The legend of the *Flying Dutchman*, a ghost ship, was incorporated into the popular *Pirates of the Caribbean* movies. People love spooky movies!

Aside from the Holy Spirit, also called the Holy Ghost, there are only two types of spirits recognized in the Scriptures—heavenly beings, called angels, who minister to the believers as God directs; and demons, fallen angelic beings, who rebelled against God and were thrown out of heaven along with Satan (also called "Lucifer").

We love angels, but our understanding of them is often incorrect. In the beloved Christmas movie *It's a Wonderful Life*, the character Clarence is an angel who had been a human and who must do an assigned good deed in order to "earn" his wings. "Teacher says every time a bell rings," says the daughter of the hero, played by Jimmy Stewart, "an angel gets its wings." Heaven is portrayed as a place where people sit on clouds and strum harps with halos over their heads.

We see angels portrayed in art—paintings, sculptures, wood, and ceramic—and we read about them in books. Many of the angels portrayed in art are females, yet every mention of angels in the Bible refers to them as males. Here are a few Scriptures that illustrate this:

> *See, I am sending an angel before you to protect you on your journey and lead you safely to the place I have prepared for you. Pay close attention to **him**, and obey **his** instructions.* (Exodus 23:20–21 NLT)

> *Then the LORD opened Balaam's eyes, and he saw the angel of the LORD standing in the roadway with a drawn sword in **his** hand.* (Numbers 22:31 NLT)

> *While [the women] were wondering about this [the empty tomb of Jesus], suddenly two **men** in clothes that gleamed like lightning stood beside them.* (Luke 24:4 NIV)

> *David looked up and saw the angel of the LORD standing between heaven and earth, with a drawn sword in **his** hand extended over Jerusalem.* (1 Chronicles 21:16 NIV)

> *Then I saw another mighty angel coming down from heaven. **He** was robed in a cloud, with a rainbow above **his** head; **his** face was like the sun, and **his** legs were like fiery pillars.* (Revelation 10:1 NIV)

Some historians think that the idea of female angels came from outside Judaism and Christianity. Many of the pagan goddesses had wings and were known for some of the actions we attribute to angels: sudden appearances, fighting battles, swordplay, carrying messages, and so on. The ancient images of Nike, the Greek goddess of victory, look a lot like the winged women we picture as angels.

Several Scriptures speak of vast numbers of angels, but only two angels are given names. Gabriel is the "Angel of Annunciation," who appeared to Mary in Nazareth and to Joseph in Luke chapter 2. Michael, the "Commander of the Host of Heaven," God's warring angel, appears in Daniel chapter 10 and in Revelation.

In Matthew 22:30, the Sadducees, who were a group of Jewish leaders, questioned Jesus about what would happen to a widow who had married seven brothers in succession—whose wife would she be in heaven? Jesus basically told them they were ignorant of the Scriptures, because those who go to heaven are *like* the angels in that they do not marry, nor are they given in marriage. (See Matthew 22:29–30.) Those who go to heaven will know their loved ones but will no longer be in families. The Scriptures tell us very clearly that we do not become ghosts after death, nor do we become angels. Man was made a little *lower* than the angels. (See Psalm 8:5.)

A story Jesus told in the gospel of Luke illustrates this point.

There was a certain rich man who was clothed in purple and fine linen and fared sumptuously every day. But there was a certain beggar named Lazarus, full of sores, who was laid at his gate, desiring to be fed with the crumbs which fell from the rich man's table. Moreover the dogs came and licked his sores. So it was that the beggar died, and was carried by the angels to Abraham's bosom. The rich man also died and was buried. And being in torments in Hades [the place of the righteous dead where those who, like Abraham, waited patiently for the Redeemer to come], he lifted up his eyes and saw Abraham afar off, and Lazarus in his bosom. Then he cried and said, "Father Abraham, have mercy on me, and send Lazarus that he may dip the tip of his finger in water and cool my tongue; for I am tormented in this flame." But Abraham said, "Son, remember that in your lifetime you received your good things, and likewise Lazarus evil things; but now he is comforted and you are tormented. And besides all this, between us and you there is a great gulf fixed, so that those who want to pass from here to you cannot, nor can those from there pass to us." (Luke 16:19–26)

The righteous dead could not go to heaven until Jesus, our Redeemer, made a way, as He did for all of us through His blood shed on the cross. Hebrews 9:27 (NIV) tells us, *"Man is destined to die once, and after that to face judgment."* No ghosts here. Thankfully, believers do not face punishment for their sins if they have been redeemed by the blood of Jesus.

Jesus was disgusted with the Jewish leaders of His day because they were hypocrites—people who said one thing and did another. He railed at them for their unbelief. *"Serpents, brood of vipers! How can you escape the condemnation of hell?"* (Matthew 23:33). For the unbeliever, there is hell. There is no in-between. There is a reason Jesus spoke of hell as many times as He spoke of heaven. I believe that He wanted us to take notice.

So, if ghosts aren't the spirits of dead people or angels, what are they? They are demonic spirits—fallen angels who seek to divert our attention off God and to themselves. They appear friendly to encourage people to communicate with them, and masquerade as spirit "guides" who come from God to give wisdom and direction. But again, they are not angelic beings from heaven; they are demon spirits.

Satan parades as an "angel of light." He can perform wonders to impress you. In John 8:44, Jesus says, *"There is no truth in him...for he is a liar and the father of lies"* (John 8:44 NIV).

The Scriptures very clearly tell us, *"In latter times some will depart from the faith, giving heed to deceiving spirits and doctrines of demons"* (1 Timothy 4:1).

As believers in Christ, we don't have to be afraid of Satan or his demon spirits. *"So we are always confident, knowing that while we are at home in the body we are absent from the Lord. For we walk by faith, not by sight. We are confident, yes, well pleased rather to be absent from the body [to be dead] and to be present with the Lord"* (2 Corinthians 5:6–8).

There is no in-between place where spirits wander aimlessly. If you know Jesus, you will see Him when you die. The spirits of those who do not know Jesus will wait to face the coming judgment when He returns.

When I read the New Testament, I am amazed to see how many times Jesus dealt with demon spirits and cast them out. Nowhere in the Scriptures does it say all the demons suddenly disappeared forever. They will remain here until the time when they, along with their leader, Satan, will face the judgment of God and be thrown into the lake of fire.

Then the devil, who had deceived them, was thrown into the fiery lake of burning sulfur, joining the beast and the false prophet. There they will be tormented day and night forever and ever. (Revelation 20:10 NLT)

11

PSYCHICS AND FORTUNE-TELLERS

After I married, my mother got involved in a group of people who claimed to be from the planet Tython. The leaders called themselves "Prince" Neosom and "Princess" Negona. Mother invited my husband and me up to the mountain community where she had provided an old-fashioned farm-house for them to live in.

I was concerned about this, but when we had dinner with them, they seemed like nice enough people—rather ordinary, in fact. I thought my fears were ungrounded. Then, after dinner, Mother announced that we were going to talk to the Lord. That presented a red flag. We didn't gather in a circle to pray; instead, my husband and I sat gingerly on the couch, while "Prince" Neasom settled himself in an easy chair, with my mother and her friends gathered around him. In a moment, he spoke in another voice, deeper than his regular one. "Good evening," he intoned.

Mother and her friends clasped their hands in joy and responded, "Good evening, Lord."

They were sure they were talking to Jesus. As "Prince" Neosom continued to speak to the group, I became extremely uncomfortable. Something was wrong here. At the time, I was unfamiliar with the practice of spirits speaking through mediums (as Patrick Swayze did via Whoopi Goldberg in *Ghost*). It just seemed strange to me, and I felt a heaviness in the room. My husband and I looked at each other, got up, and beat a hasty retreat from the house.

Later, my mother, still heavily involved in this group, cautioned me, saying that a spaceship might land on the playground of the school where I was teaching. She told me that when that happened, I was to calmly lead my class into the spaceship to save them. Her group believed that two spaceships were holding the earth on its axis. The group advanced other unusual teachings, and I prayed that my mother would see the light and somehow escape their clutches.

Later, as I began to read about this unseen world and about spirit possession, I realized that the man called "Prince" Neosom was channeling a familiar spirit, a demon spirit, and it was not the Lord to whom they were talking.

In many cities, there are individuals who make a living as "psychics." Along with claiming to foretell the future, these people take advantage of the bereaved who are missing a deceased loved one so badly that they are compelled to consult a psychic in hopes of hearing from him.

Demons have been around since Satan first defied and rebelled against God, resulting in his being cast out of heaven, along with one third of the angels, who had followed him in rebellion. In the thousands of years since the rebellion, these fallen angels, now demon spirits, have learned much about your ancestors and your life. They are perfectly capable of giving this information to mediums or psychics who serve them.

When I was young, I read several books by Edgar Cayce and Jeane Dixon, two well-known psychics in their day. I thought they were remarkable, and it wasn't until I was older and had done some research that I learned how they got their power.

Sometimes in tearooms, a woman will offer to "read" your tea leaves and tell you your fortune. At many Halloween carnivals and fairs, women dressed as gypsies sit at tables with a crystal ball, waiting to tell passersby their future.

This art of "seeing" is called "scrying," when images are supposedly seen in the crystal. This information is then often used to help a person make important decisions in his or her life, as in the areas of love, marriage, finances, and so forth.

When scrying is used with crystals or a transparent body, it is called "crystallomancy" or "crystal gazing."

According to *Roget's 21st Century Thesaurus*, other terms for fortune-teller include "medium," "seer," "clairvoyant," "augur," "crystal ball gazer," "diviner," "palmist," "prophet," "tarot reader," and "tea-leaf reader."[18]

---

18. fortune-teller. Thesaurus.com. *Roget's 21st Century Thesaurus, Third Edition*. Philip Lief Group 2009. http://thesaurus.com/browse/fortune-teller (accessed: April 23, 2014).

One of the synonyms for *psychic* is *prophet*, yet a psychic is anything but a prophet. Prophets of the Bible are quite different from these people who claim to have received wisdom from God. Great prophets in the Bible, like Elijah and Elisha, had supernatural powers granted them by God through the indwelling Holy Spirit. The special information they gave to the Israelites was from God, not from evil spirits. The prophets in the Scriptures were obedient to God's will, and many times, the words they were given were to warn the people or, as in the case of Daniel, were supernatural glimpses into what God was going to do in the future. The important distinction is the Bible gives us a tests to see if someone who claims to be a prophet is from God.

> *Dear friends, do not believe every spirit, but test the spirits to see whether they are from God, because many false prophets have gone out into the world. This is how you can recognize the Spirit of God: Every spirit that acknowledges that Jesus Christ has come in the flesh is from God, but every spirit that does not acknowledge Jesus is not from God. This is the spirit of the antichrist, which you have heard is coming and even now is already in the world.* (1 John 4:1–3 NIV)

Once again, we can go to the Scriptures for a fuller understanding of psychics. In Isaiah 8:19 (NIV), we read,

> *When men tell you to consult mediums and spiritists, who whisper and mutter, should not a people inquire of their God? Why consult the dead on behalf of the living?*

If you wonder whether psychics or fortune-tellers receive their power from God, ask them if they follow Jesus Christ and are saved by the blood He shed on the cross. You may be surprised at their response.

In the book of Zechariah, God says, *"Household gods give worthless advice, fortune-tellers predict only lies, and interpreters of dreams pronounce falsehoods that give no comfort"* (Zechariah 10:2 NLT). The prophesies of Edgar Cayce and Jeane Dixon occasionally came true, giving them some credence; but, more often than not, their predictions came to nothing. Surprisingly, many people still hung on their every word.

God also says, *"I will set my face against the person who turns to mediums and spiritists to prostitute himself by following them, and I will cut him off from his people"* (Leviticus 20:6 NIV). Those are pretty strong words.

Another means of divination is tarot cards. Fortune-tellers use them to predict a person's future. As early as I can remember, my mother entertained her friends by telling them their fortunes using tarot cards. She used a regular deck of playing cards and would lay them down in a hexagonal shape. The pattern that emerged as she turned them over determined that person's "fortune." All I remember now is that the ace of spades meant death, and the ten of hearts meant marriage. When I was old enough, my mother taught me how to read the cards, and I would tell my own fortune each morning. If it wasn't very good or showed something bad, I would repeat the pattern again and again until the result was better.

Once again, this practice of depending on cards to tell our future is wrong; it keeps us from depending on our loving God. Using any kind of man-made method this way is wrong in God's eyes.

"Palmistry," or "chiromancy," is the art or practice of interpreting a person's character or predicting his future by examining the lines and other features of his hand, especially his palm and fingers. By this practice, a palm reader tells a person whether he will have a long life, find the woman of his dreams, have a happy marriage, become wealthy, and so forth.

Palmistry began in the Far East. It was a method of counseling that originated in India more than three thousand years ago and was later used in China, Persia (modern-day Iran), Tibet, and some European countries. Ancient peoples like the Hindus, Sumerians, Tibetans, Hebrews, and Babylonians were very good at this art. Many famous figures of history, including Homer, Socrates, and Napoleon, were said to have popularized the laws and practice of palmistry—a method of seeking to know the future from the powers of darkness rather than from the living God. Alexander the Great became very interested in palmistry and used the method to examine the character of his officers.

During the Middle Ages, the Catholic Church strongly discouraged palmistry, calling it a pagan superstition. During the Renaissance, palmistry was classified as one of the seven "forbidden arts," along with necromancy (communicating with the dead to determine the future) and other occult practices.

In 1889, the Chirological Society of Great Britain was founded in London by Katherine St. Hill. Her aim was to advance the art of palmistry and prevent any abuse of the art. Another famous figure in the palmistry movement was the Irishman William John Warner. He went by the name "Cheiro," which is derived from "cheiromancy"—another spelling of the term. Some of Warner's famous clients included Mark Twain, Sarah Bernhardt, Edward VIII (Prince of Wales), U.S. president Grover Cleveland, and Thomas Edison, among others. Mark Twain wrote, "Cheiro has exposed my character to me with humiliating accuracy. I ought not to confess this accuracy, still I am moved to do it."

Another form of seeing into the future involves the use of crystals. Professed "seers" say they don't actually see images in the crystals themselves, but that the clearness of the stones enables them to clear their minds of distractions, so that the "truths" can become known to them.

Noted British mathematician, astronomer, astrologer, and geographer Dr. John Dee, a consultant to Queen Elizabeth I, devoted his life to divination and other occult practices, and was known for his use of crystal balls.

Crystal balls have been used in feng shui, "a Chinese geomantic practice in which a structure or site is chosen or configured so as to harmonize with the spiritual forces that inhabit it." It is used to clear a room of energy so as to soothe people. Some businessmen and women feel that when feng shui is used in a meeting, it smoothes the chaotic energy of competition and makes them feel more productive. Have you had someone organize your home or business according to feng shui?

The crystal ball is said to exude occult energy and power, and psychics use them to supposedly uncover mysteries they reveal to their clients. They believe crystal balls help them see into the future and uncover the mysteries of the past. It provides a "window into another dimension." The dimension is spiritual, indeed, but the spirits are demonic. Psychics and others who use crystal balls do not get their powers from God.

Today's psychics are usually New Agers, following a movement that is a far cry from Christianity. Psychics gather their information from evil spirits and the dead. In biblical times, people who professed to have God's spirit of prophecy and were found to be false were stoned to death. Let us not fall into the temptation to use or to consult such forms of divination.

12

WITCHES

In the later 1960s, I attended a Christian women's luncheon. The featured speaker, a beautiful young woman, was a former witch. Her family had been into witchcraft, and her father was a male witch. (Male witches are sometimes called warlocks, but that term is considered derogatory by many.)

Our speaker had renounced the world of witchcraft to become a Christian. During her talk, we innocent house-wives sat glued to our chairs as she told us what was going on in our own city—that there were over forty temples of satanic worship. Gasps arose all over the room.

As a child, this girl and her friends would go into the bathroom at school and conjure up spirits in the mirror. She told of fifteen hundred kids who climbed Cowles Mountain in San Diego to watch a small group of satanic believers sacrifice a goat. We were shocked, fascinated, and appalled. Nowhere in our ordered lives had we any inkling of that other world.

When most of us think of witches, our minds conjure up a woman with a hooked nose (usually with a wart); a black outfit; a tall, pointed black hat; and a broom. Some of us may think of the Wicked Witch of the East or of Glinda, the good witch, from *The Wizard of Oz*. Is there a difference? Are there really two kinds of witches?

Merriam-Webster's 11th Collegiate Dictionary defines *witch* as "a woman practicing usually black witchcraft often with the aid of a devil or a familiar [spirit]."

Exodus 22:18 says, *"You shall not permit a sorceress to live."* *Sorceress* is another name for *witch*. In Deuteronomy 18:10, God clearly says,

> *There shall not be found among you anyone…who practices witchcraft, or a soothsayer, or one who interprets omens, or a sorcerer, or one who conjures spells, or a medium, or a spiritist, or one who calls up the dead. For all who do these things are an abomination to the LORD.*

In the Scriptures, an abomination is something that is offensive to God, something that makes Him angry. This includes turning to occult things, like those listed above, instead of turning to Him.

The religion practiced by witches is called Wicca. To women and men who practice Wicca and meet in groups called "covens," Halloween is considered a sacred occasion.

The Wiccan book *Neopaganism* celebrates three special dates for witchcraft:

Their "sabbats," or festivals, include (1) Samhain, the Celtic New Year, celebrated on Halloween and November 1; (2) Oimelc, a purification festival, celebrated on February 1; and (3) Beltane, a fertility festival, celebrated on May 1.[19] Witches, like other religious groups, expect a day off work for observance of their "religious" holiday, which is Halloween.

Many kings of Israel did wicked things and dabbled in the occult. One of the most evil kings, Manasseh, practiced soothsaying, or fortune-telling, used witchcraft and sorcery, and consulted mediums and spiritists. The Scriptures say that he did much evil in the sight of the Lord and provoked Him to anger. During Manasseh's reign, pagan gods were worshipped heavily, and the Israelites fell away from the true God, practicing every form of evil.

Israel's first king, Saul, was very handsome and stood taller than most men. When first anointed king, he was a shy and humble man who hid from the prophet Samuel, afraid of the enormous responsibility the prophet would bestow on him. Samuel found him and explained to the people all the things a king required, including young men for his army and taxes for the kingdom.

Saul may have started out humble, but as he began to win battles and gain power, he became proud. One day, the prophet Samuel, who had anointed him as king, told him to go and destroy the Amalekites, a wicked people. God had given them four hundred years to repent, but they had grown so evil, practicing wickedness and the occult, that they were not to be spared. Saul's army captured the city, but Saul disregarded Samuel's instructions to destroy every living thing

19. Margot Alder, quoted in Ankerberg et al., *Facts on Halloween*, 27.

that dwelled there. He did not do what God had commanded him to do. Saul not only spared the wicked king of the city; he also took spoil from the city and saved many of the animals, such as the sheep and donkeys, for himself.

When Samuel discovered what Saul had done, he was angry. Saul told him that he had saved the animals as a sacrifice to God, but Samuel told him, *"To obey is better than sacrifice"* (1 Samuel 15:22). God's Spirit was removed from Saul, and Samuel told him his kingdom would be given to his rival, David. No longer in God's favor, Saul was vulnerable to the wiles of the devil, and the Scriptures tell us that an evil spirit came upon him. Let's look at what happened next:

> *Now Samuel had died, and all Israel had lamented for him and buried him in Ramah, in his own city. And Saul had put the mediums and the spiritists out of the land. Then the Philistines gathered together, and came and encamped at Shunem. So Saul gathered all Israel together, and they encamped at Gilboa. When Saul saw the army of the Philistines, he was afraid, and his heart trembled greatly.* (1 Samuel 28:3–5)

The Philistine army was almost twice the size of Saul's army, and Saul feared them.

> *And when Saul inquired of the* LORD, *the* LORD *did not answer him, either by dreams or by Urim or by the prophets. Then Saul said to his servants, "Find me a woman who is a medium* [someone who calls upon the dead to commune with them], *that I may go to her and inquire of her."* (1 Samuel 28:6–7)

Like Saul, when we are greatly afraid, sometimes we do the wrong thing. Saul's decision wasn't wise. He had sent all the mediums and spiritists away, but he still was disobeying God. Let's see what happened next.

And his servants said to him, "In fact, there is a woman who is a medium at En Dor." So Saul disguised himself and put on other clothes, and he went, and two men with him; and they came to the woman by night. And he said, "Please conduct a seance for me, and bring up for me the one I shall name to you." Then the woman said to him, "Look, you know what Saul has done, how he has cut off the mediums and the spiritists from the land. Why then do you lay a snare for my life, to cause me to die?" And Saul swore to her by the LORD, saying, "As the LORD lives, no punishment shall come upon you for this thing." Then the woman said, "Whom shall I bring up for you?" And he said, "Bring up Samuel for me." When the woman saw Samuel, she cried out with a loud voice. And the woman spoke to Saul, saying, "Why have you deceived me? For you are Saul!" And the king said to her, "Do not be afraid. What did you see?" And the woman said to Saul, "I saw a spirit ascending out of the earth." So he said to her, "What is his form?" And she said, "An old man is coming up, and he is covered with a mantle." And Saul perceived that it was Samuel, and he stooped with his face to the ground and bowed down. Now Samuel said to Saul, "Why have you disturbed me by bringing me up?" (1 Samuel 28:7–15)

Samuel was waiting in Sheol, because Jesus had not yet come to bring salvation and open the door to the kingdom of heaven. The spirits of the righteous dead who were waiting for the promise of God waited in Sheol, which had two parts: paradise (Sheol) and torment (Hades), as mentioned earlier in the story of Lazarus the beggar.

And Saul answered, "I am deeply distressed; for the Philistines make war against me, and God has departed from me and does not answer me anymore, neither by prophets nor by dreams. Therefore I have called you, that you may reveal to me what I should do." Then Samuel said: "Why then do you ask me, seeing the LORD has departed from you and has become your enemy? And the LORD has done for Himself as He spoke by me. For the LORD has torn the kingdom out of your hand and given it to your neighbor, David. (1 Samuel 28:15–17)

Samuel scolded Saul for trusting in a witch instead of the living God, and told him he and his sons would die in battle the next day. And his prophecy came true. Saul and his sons were slain in battle, and David became king of Israel.

Ephesians 4:8–9 tells us, *"When [Jesus] ascended on high, He led captivity captive….(Now this, "He ascended"; what does it mean but that He also first descended into the lower parts of the earth?)"*

After the resurrection, the righteous dead aren't in Sheol anymore. When Jesus died, He went to the paradise side of Hades and "took captivity captive." He took the souls of the righteous, such as the souls of Abraham, Sarah, Jacob, and Samuel, to heaven with Him. Matthew 12:40 says, *"For as Jonah was three days and three nights in the belly of the great fish, so will the Son of Man be three days and three nights in the heart of the earth."* And Acts 2:27 says, *"You will not leave my soul in Hades, nor will You allow Your Holy One to see corruption."*

Again, witches, like the one in En Dor, practice Wicca, an earth-centered religion. Wicca has also been called "The Craft" or "The Old Religion," claiming that the world is a living, breathing organism and that people are "gods" or "goddesses." Wiccans practice magick, which is spelled differently to avoid confusing it with "magic," something they contend is used purely for entertainment. Their motto is, "If it harms none, do as ye will." They believe that moral and religious truths are relative.

Contrary to the musical *Wicked* and the movie *The Wizard of Oz*, there are no "good" witches. Perhaps some people confuse a "good witch" with a "white witch." White witchcraft is the worship of Mother Nature. Adherents say that they do not use their craft for evil, believing that whatever they send out comes back threefold. They profess to do only "good" magic. Yet there is no such thing as "good" magic; God clearly tells us that sorcerers and magicians who practice magic are an abomination to Him.

I wanted to know more about white witches, so I read an interview with a young woman, a "white witch," named Lucy Walton. She defined white witchcraft this way: "White witchcraft means you worship Mother Nature; the Earth, the Goddess, and the God. Witches celebrate all that the earth is and the cycles of the year....You tune yourself into nature and use the elements around you; the planets, the sun, moon, herbs, flowers, trees, crystals, and colours. This will all help in your spell work."[20]

She also said, "Thanks to a lot of modern films and books like *Harry Potter*, [people are beginning to believe] that witches are normal everyday people and it takes a lot of hard work."[21] Furthermore, "The explosive growth of the Harry Potter children's book series and the related popularity of similar books and films has also increased cultural acceptance of such pagan beliefs."[22]

20. http://www.femalefirst.co.uk/culture/White+Witches-251324.html.
21. Ibid.
22. Ankerberg et al., *Facts on Halloween*, 27.

In his book series The Chronicles of Narnia, C. S. Lewis named one of the villains the "White Witch," challenging the image of white witchcraft as good.

In 1973, a woman named Doreen Irvine published her autobiography, *From Witchcraft to Christ*, in which she states, "Witchcraft of the black kind is not far removed from Satanism...Black witches have great power and are not to be taken lightly."[23] Just like the Druids, they offer human sacrifices. Irvine also claimed that forty-seven demons were exorcised from her body. She also used the terms "witchcraft" and "Satanism" as if they were one and the same.

In the early modern era in Europe, people who practiced folk magic didn't think of themselves as witches but as healers or seers. Nevertheless, they were convicted of practicing witchcraft. Some English "witches" were convicted of working with demons. In Hungary, many of the alleged witches were considered healers; others considered themselves mediators between the spiritual worlds. They believed in contacting fairies, spirits, or the dead, and claimed to have out-of-body experiences—traveling to "other worlds." Many times, stories of those accused of witchcraft shared common themes, such as the person participating in processions of the dead or presiding over large feasts. These people also claimed to fight evil spirits, "vampires," or witches, and to bring prosperity to their people. Good or bad, the prevailing "judges" sentenced these people to be burned at the stake.

Many satanic groups consider Halloween a special night because it is a time when they can call upon the devil to inquire of the future. These groups claim to receive insights into the events of the following year, including upcoming harvests, marriages, deaths, and so forth.

---

23. Doreen Irvine, *From Witchcraft to Christ*, quoted in Ankerberg et al., *Facts on Halloween*, 28.

Witchcraft and Satanism are two different movements, but they are both led by Satan himself, who strengthens them to accomplish his purposes.

As a Christian, I know that I need to consider what God's Word says regarding witches. *"Beloved, do not imitate what is evil, but what is good. He who does good is of God, but he who does evil has not seen God"* (3 John 1:11). Knowing this, I believe we should not dress as witches or allow our children to dress as them on Halloween. Participating in Halloween by dressing our children in costume and allowing them to interact with other children dressed as witches is an imitation of what God says is evil. And while our children may not be practicing Wiccans, exposing them to witch-related things may make them more open to the occult in later years. My childhood was filled with elements of spiritual darkness, which made me vulnerable to the enemy, who dominated my life for many years.

First Thessalonians 5:22 (NIV) tells us to *"avoid every kind of evil."* Notice the word *"every."* If you had to describe the customs of Halloween, how would you describe them? Is there anything about Halloween that is good?

First John 1:5–6 (NIV) says, *"This is the message we have heard from him and declare to you: God is light; in him there is no darkness at all. If we claim to have fellowship with him yet walk in the darkness, we lie and do not live by the truth."*

These are strong words and raise the question, Is partaking in Halloween walking in the darkness or the light? As we submit this question to the Lord, we can be sure that He will lead us in the way we should go.

CLOSING THE DOOR ON SATAN

How does all the information I have shared thus far affect Halloween as we celebrate it today? Each of these subjects—black cats, owls, jack-o'-lanterns, ghosts, witches, zombies—represents an area of the occult, which is hardly an innocuous realm. We have morphed Halloween into a seemingly harmless holiday for children and adults. We make things that are an abomination to the Lord of no consequence as we teach our children that Halloween is just a fun day to dress up and collect candy from neighbors, giving no thought to whom and what we are actually celebrating.

When my daughter was in grade school, she had a sleepover with some of her friends. I came downstairs to bring them a snack and found them gathered around one girl who was lying on the floor. Each of the other girls had put one finger under her, and at my startled exclamation, "What are you doing?" they told me they were going to "levitate" her, or cause her body to rise up from the floor.

I put a stop to that right away, for I knew that the power of levitation came from Satan. The girls had no idea that it was wrong. They had learned the practice from friends and thought it was just a fun thing to do. We do a lot of things because they seem fun.

The devil is not in it merely for fun. The Scriptures tell us that he *"walks about like a roaring lion, seeking whom he may devour"* (1 Peter 5:8). You enter his world, no matter how innocent it seems, and he has power over you.

If you've given your heart to Jesus, you will want to consider the consequences of celebrating Halloween. Will there be jack-o'-lanterns on your porch and ghosts, goblins, and witches in your front lawn? Will your children dress in costumes? As my research and personal experience reflect, Halloween is not a hallowed eve but a night that belongs to Satan and his minions. When you enter the enemy's territory, you give him certain rights. You open the door to his minions, his demon spirits.

When we align ourselves with anything connected to evil spirits, we are deeply affected. Why become involved with things that God says He hates, which dishonor His name? Halloween is a day of dark powers and evil, a day chosen by the ancient Druids and still celebrated by modern-day witches and Satanists. Most of us have lived totally unaware of these facts for years. As believers, we want to glorify God;

so we must ask ourselves if we want to observe something that began as a pagan holiday.

If we want to avoid the appearance of evil, as the Scriptures direct us to (see 1 Thessalonians 5:22 KJV), perhaps we shouldn't send our children trick-or-treating dressed as zombies, devils, witches, or ghosts.

Some people think that since they do not believe in those ancient rites and practices, they are innocent of any evil. But merely not believing in something does not make it go away.

Third John chapter 1:11 exhorts, *"Do not imitate what is evil, but what is good."* Are we giving credence to the day most related to evil spirits by celebrating Halloween? Children love Halloween. They delight in stories of witches, ghosts, goblins, zombies, and monsters. However, we are admonished to imitate Christ, not the practices of the enemy. This should be the foundation of what we teach our children. *"Hate what is evil; cling to what is good"* (Romans 12:9 NIV). *"Avoid every kind of evil"* (1 Thessalonians 5:22 NIV).

Again, if we are children of the light, how can we associate with the things of darkness? (See Ephesians 5:8.)

You can no longer protest ignorance as to the origins of Halloween. With all this knowledge, do you think that God is pleased to look down from heaven and see His children's children dressed as witches, ghosts, and devils? We are the ones He died for, breaking the bonds of Satan, and here we are, honoring that same evil one. Throughout history, Halloween has been a night in which human children have been sacrificed. Knowing who Satan is, what he stands for, and how he sees Halloween, will you send your children out on such an evening?

Jesus loved little children. When His disciples wanted to shoo them away, He rebuked them and said, *"Let the little children come to Me, and do not forbid them; for of such is the kingdom of heaven"* (Matthew 19:14). Didn't He say, *"Whoever causes one of these little ones who believe in me to sin, it would be better for him to be thrown into the sea with a large millstone tied around his neck"* (Mark 9:42 NIV)? When we consider allowing our children to participate in Halloween, we should consider these words. I'm not shaking my finger and accusing believers of sinning if they celebrate Halloween, but I would encourage us to ask ourselves, "Are we honoring God?"

Let us consider some additional questions:

1. Will our or our children's participation in Halloween influence our neighbors, friends, and family members?

2. How many Christians actually know the origins of Halloween?

3. Are we ignorantly copying something that is evil?

4. Keeping in mind 1 Corinthians 10:23–24 (NIV), *"'Everything is permissible'—but not everything is beneficial. 'Everything is permissible'—but not everything is constructive. Nobody should seek his own good, but the good of others,"* should we do as we please, regardless of how it affects others?

REFERENCES

Ankerberg, John, John Weldon, and Dillon Burroughs, *The Facts on Halloween*. Eugene, OR: Harvest House Publishers, 1996, 2008.

Bannatyne, Lesley. *Halloween: An American Holiday, an American History*. Gretna, LA: Pelican Publishing Company, 1990, 1998.

Browne, Sylvia. *The Truth About Psychics: What's Real, What's Not, and How to Tell the Difference*. New York, NY: Fireside, 2009.

James, Simon. *Exploring the World of the Celts*. London: Thames & Hudson, 1993.

Morton, Lisa. *Trick or Treat? A History of Halloween*. London: Reaktion Books Ltd., 2012.

Rosalind Beimler in Greenleigh, John. *The Days of the Dead*. San Francisco, CA: Pomegranate Communications, 1998.

ABOUT THE AUTHOR

Diana Wallis Taylor was first published at the age of twelve, when she sold a poem to a church newsletter. Today, she has an extensive portfolio of published works, including a collection of poetry; an Easter cantata, written with a musical collaborator; contributions to various magazines and compilations; and six award-winning novels, including five biblical fiction stories: *Ruth, Mother of Kings*; *Journey to the Well* (the story of the woman of Samaria); *Martha*; *Mary Magdalene*; and *Claudia, Wife of Pontius Pilate*.

Diana lives in San Diego with her husband, Frank. Among them, they have six grown children and nine grandchildren. Readers can learn more by visiting her Web site, www.dianawallistaylor.com.